The Answers You Seek

Are Within

Amanda Clarke, the visionary author behind "Divine Guidance: Answers from the Oracles" is a spiritual guide and luminary dedicated to illuminating the paths of seekers with cosmic wisdom. This book is a testament to Amanda's profound connection with the universe and her mission to provide a simple yet potent tool for accessing divine guidance.

With a rich background in spirituality, mysticism, and personal growth, Amanda brings a depth of understanding to her work. "Answers from the Oracles" is a reflection of her own transformative journey, where the whispers of the cosmos have been her guiding light. Beyond a mere collection of answers, the book serves as a conduit for readers to establish a direct link with the universe.

In the author's notes, Amanda emphasizes the sacred connection readers can forge with the book. It transcends being a mere guide; it becomes a spiritual companion, attuned to the unique energy of each seeker. Amanda encourages a process of simplicity - holding, meditating, and infusing energy into the pages, making the book a personalized and intimate experience.

As readers flip through these blessed pages of "Divine Guidance: Answers from the Oracles." Amanda's hope is for each seeker to find solace, clarity, and inspiration. The book, more than a mere guide, stands as an invitation to connect with the divine, navigate life's questions, and embark on a transformative journey toward self-discovery.

Namaste - The divine in me honors the divine in you.

More on the Bookshelves at www.korupublishing.com

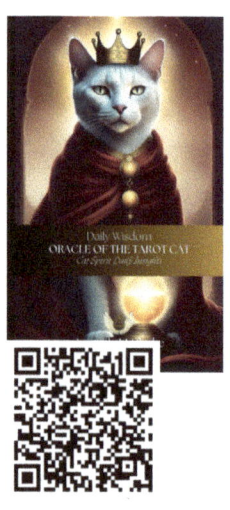

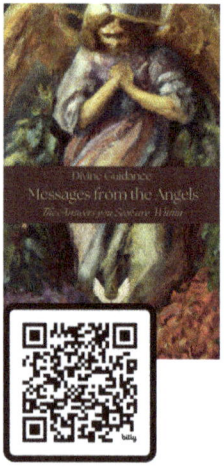

Divine Guidance
ANSWERS FROM THE ORACLES
Guidance and Inspiration from Divine Oracles

Amanda M Clarke

KORU PUBLISING

KORU (Maori:NZ): A symbol of spiritual growth and spiritual connection.

First Edition

In this inaugural edition of 'Divine Guidance: Answers from the Oracles,' embark on a profound journey where instant cosmic insights await, offering swift and unequivocal answers to your burning questions. This divination tool transcends the ordinary, serving as a sacred conduit between you and the universe, inviting you to tap into the profound wisdom nestled within its pages.

Divine Guidance: Answers from the Oracles,' in its first edition, stands as your steadfast companion on the odyssey of self discovery, offering swift and reliable cosmic responses to illuminate your path with divine wisdom. As you connect, inquire, and engage with the pages, let the universe unravel its secrets, guiding you toward the profound revelations that await.

Copyright © 2024 by Koru Lifestylist

All rights reserved. All content, materials, and intellectual property in this book or any other platform owned by Koru Lifestylist are protected by copyright laws. This includes text, images, graphics, videos, audio, software, and any other form of content that may be produced by Koru Lifestylist.

No part of this content may be reproduced, distributed, or transmitted in any form or by any means without the prior written permission of Koru Lifestylist. This means that you cannot copy, reproduce, or use any of the content in this book for commercial or personal purposes without the express written consent of Koru Lifestylist.

Unauthorized use of any copyrighted material owned by Koru Lifestylist may result in legal action being taken against you. Koru Lifestylist reserves the right to pursue all available legal remedies against any individual or entity found to be infringing on its copyright.

In summary, Koru Lifestylist © 2024 holds exclusive rights to all the content produced by it, and any unauthorized use of such content will result in legal action.

My Dearest Amelia,

As I sit down to write these words, my heart swells with love and pride for the incredible young woman you've become. You've always been my inspiration, my guiding light, and it is for you that I've embarked on this journey of writing.

Seeing your unwavering quest for answers, your thirst for understanding, and your courage to navigate life's twists and turns fills me with awe. You, my dear daughter, are the embodiment of resilience, curiosity, and grace.

It is your insatiable hunger for knowledge, your relentless pursuit of truth, that has fueled my own exploration into the realms of the divine and the mysteries of the universe. You have shown me the beauty of curiosity, the power of seeking, and the importance of trusting in the journey.

As I pen these words, know that you are my inspiration, my motivation, and my greatest teacher. Your journey is my journey, and together, we shall continue to seek, to learn, and to grow.

May this book serve as a beacon of light on your path, guiding you with divine wisdom and clarity. Know that I am always here for you, cheering you on every step of the way.

With all my love,

Mum xxx

Disclaimer: This Divine Guidance: Answers from the Oracles book provides information on spiritual readings and interpretation, but it is not intended as a substitute for professional advice, diagnosis, or treatment. The information contained in this book is provided for educational and entertainment purposes only and is not meant to be taken as specific advice for individual circumstances. The author and publisher make no representations or warranties with respect to the accuracy or completeness of the contents of this book and specifically disclaim any implied warranties of merchantability or fitness for a particular purpose. The reader should always consult with a licensed professional for any specific concerns or questions. The author and publisher shall not be liable for any loss or damage caused or alleged to have been caused, directly or indirectly, by the information contained in this book. The use of this book is at the reader's sole risk

Using the Book

Welcome to Your Journey

"Divine Guidance: Answers from the Oracles" is not just a book: it's a portal to deeper insight and connection with the divine energies that surround us. This guide will assist you in unlocking the wisdom within its pages, allowing divine guidance to illuminate your path and answer your questions.

Cleanse the Book

This book has passed through many hands to reach you. Your first use you need to cleanse all old energies that this book may have picked up on its' way to you. This ritual should be performed before using your book for the first time and again at regular intervals, especially if you do readings for other people.

1. Stand barefoot in nature, on the earth.
2. Hold the book out in front on your non-dominant hand, palm facing up.
3. With your dominant hand in a fist, knock 3 times on the book. This action will remove all energies from the book to the earth below.
4. Imbibe the book with your own energies by

flipping through the book, touching every page and saying this incantation:

"In divine light, I hold you near,
Removing all that's dark,
bringing clarity clear.
May your pages shine with purest grace,
Guiding seekers to their rightful place."

Preparing Your Sacred Space
1. Find a Quiet Sanctuary: Select a tranquil space where you can focus without distractions. Create an atmosphere of peace and serenity to enhance your connection with the divine energies.
2. Clear the Book's Energy: You may use sage, palo santo, or your preferred cleansing method to purify the book's energy. Lightly pass the smoke around the book, setting the intention to release any stagnant or negative energies and inviting in divine guidance.
3. Set Your Intention: Hold the book in your hands and take a moment to center yourself. Close your eyes, take a few deep breaths, and set a clear intention to receive divine guidance and clarity. Visualize your question or intention as a

beam of light emanating from your heart and infusing the book with your energy.

Connecting with Divine Guidance

1. Flip Through the Pages: With your intention set, gently flip through the pages of the book. Trust your intuition and allow your inner guidance to direct your movements.

2. Stop and Focus: When you feel guided to stop, pause and focus on the page before you. Trust that the divine energies have led you to the message that holds the guidance or answer you seek.

3. Receive the Guidance: Take your time to read and absorb the message on the page. Pay attention to any thoughts, feelings, or sensations that arise within you. Trust that the divine wisdom is speaking directly to your soul.

4. Reflect and Apply: Reflect on how the message resonates with your question or situation. Consider how you can apply the guidance received to navigate your path with clarity and purpose.

5. Express Gratitude: Conclude your practice by expressing gratitude for the divine guidance received. Thank the universe, your guides, and the book itself for the insights and clarity provided.

Repeat this process as often as needed, allowing the divine guidance to support you on your journey of growth, transformation, and spiritual awakening. Trust in the wisdom of the oracles and know that you are always supported and guided by the divine energies that surround you.

Journalling Pages
In the "Divine Guidance: Answers from the Oracles" book, every reading page is accompanied by its own dedicated journal page! This space is specially designed for you to capture your thoughts, emotions, and experiences during your readings. Remember to date each entry and jot down a brief sentence—it's akin to leaving a trace of your journey in this enchanted book of moments!

The Answers You Seek

Are Within

My daily thoughts....

Radiate love

Embrace the profound truth that love is the universal language that transcends barriers and elevates the collective consciousness. By radiating love from the depths of your being, you not only uplift your own spirit but also create a ripple effect of positivity and harmony in the world around you.

My daily thoughts....

Trust your inner guidance

Within the depths of your soul lies an innate wisdom that knows the way forward. Trust in the whispers of your intuition, for they are the divine compass guiding you along your path of purpose and fulfillment.

My daily thoughts....

Embrace the unknown

Embrace the mysteries of life with open arms, for within the unknown lies infinite potential and endless possibilities waiting to unfold.

My daily thoughts....

Cultivate a grateful heart

Shift your focus from scarcity to abundance by cultivating a heart overflowing with gratitude for the blessings, both big and small, that grace your life each day.

My daily thoughts....

Release the need for approval

Free yourself from the shackles of seeking validation from others and instead embrace your inherent worth and uniqueness.

My daily thoughts....

Surrender to divine timing

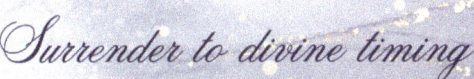

Trust that everything unfolds in divine order and that the universe has a perfect plan for you. Surrendering to the flow of divine timing allows you to release resistance and embrace the unfolding of your destiny with grace and ease.

My daily thoughts....

Express your creativity freely

Tap into the wellspring of creativity that resides within you and allow your unique gifts and talents to shine brightly.

My daily thoughts....

Trust in your resilience

Draw upon the strength and resilience that lies within you to overcome life's challenges and emerge stronger and more empowered than ever before.

My daily thoughts....

Find joy in simple pleasures

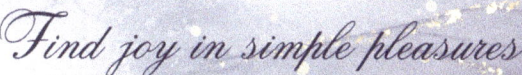

Cultivate a sense of childlike wonder and find joy in the beauty of life's simple pleasures, from a breathtaking sunset to a heartfelt conversation with a loved one.

My daily thoughts....

Connect with your inner child

Reconnect with the innocence, curiosity, and spontaneity of your inner child and allow their playful spirit to infuse your life with joy and wonder.

My daily thoughts....

Choose love in the face of adversity

In every moment, you have the power to choose love over fear, kindness over judgment, and compassion over indifference.

My daily thoughts....

Honor your journey

Embrace the journey you've traveled thus far, honoring the lessons learned, the growth experienced, and the resilience gained along the way.

My daily thoughts....

See challenges as stepping stones

View challenges as opportunities for growth and transformation, recognizing that each obstacle you encounter is ultimately leading you closer to your highest potential and greatest fulfillment.

My daily thoughts....

Trust in the unfolding of your destiny

Have faith that the universe is guiding you toward your highest good and that everything is unfolding exactly as it should. Trust in the divine timing of your life's journey and remain open to the infinite possibilities that await you.

My daily thoughts....

Let go of attachments to outcomes

Release the need to control every aspect of your life and instead surrender to the flow of the universe. Trust that the universe has a plan for you and that everything is happening for your highest good, even if it doesn't always seem that way in the moment.

My daily thoughts....

Embrace the ebb and flow of life's energy

Recognize that life is filled with ups and downs, highs and lows, and that each experience serves to shape and mold you into the person you are meant to become. Embrace the fluctuations of life's energy and trust that, like the tide, it will always ebb and flow in perfect harmony with the universe.

My daily thoughts....

Practice mindfulness

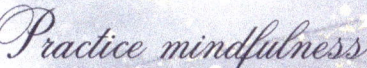

Cultivate a state of present-moment awareness by focusing your attention on the here and now. Practice mindfulness in your daily life by bringing your full attention to each task, each breath, and each moment, allowing you to experience a deeper sense of peace and connection with the world around you.

My daily thoughts....

Celebrate your accomplishments

Take time to acknowledge and celebrate your achievements, both big and small, recognizing the hard work, dedication, and perseverance that went into each success. By celebrating your accomplishments, you not only boost your self-esteem and confidence but also cultivate a positive mindset that attracts even more success into your life.

My daily thoughts....

Release the need for validation from others

Free yourself from the need to seek approval or validation from others and instead validate yourself from within. Recognize your own worth and value, independent of the opinions or judgments of others, and trust that your worthiness is inherent simply because you exist.

My daily thoughts....

Embrace vulnerability

Allow yourself to be authentic and vulnerable, recognizing that true strength lies in embracing your imperfections and allowing yourself to be seen exactly as you are. By embracing vulnerability, you open yourself up to deeper connections, greater intimacy, and a more authentic and fulfilling life.

My daily thoughts....

Trust in the power of your dreams

Believe in the power of your dreams and aspirations, trusting that they are not merely wishful thinking but powerful manifestations of your deepest desires and highest potential. Trust in your ability to turn your dreams into reality and take inspired action toward making them come true.

My daily thoughts....

Listen to your body's wisdom

Tune into the signals and messages that your body sends you, recognizing that it is constantly communicating with you in subtle ways. Listen to your body's wisdom and honor its needs and desires, trusting that it knows what is best for you and guiding you toward optimal health and well-being.

My daily thoughts....

Find joy in simple pleasures; they are treasures.

Amidst the hustle and bustle of life, it's easy to overlook the simple pleasures that bring joy to our hearts. Take time to savor the beauty of life's small moments, finding delight in the everyday wonders that surround you, and treasure each moment as a precious gift to be cherished.

My daily thoughts....

Connect with your inner child;
it brings joy.

The inner child within you holds the key to boundless joy, creativity, and wonder. Reconnect with your inner child, embracing their playful spirit, curiosity, and imagination, and rediscover the joy and magic of life through the eyes of innocence and pure-heartedness.

My daily thoughts....

Accept peace in the face of adversity.

Love is the most potent antidote to fear, hatred, and darkness, transcending all barriers and transforming even the most challenging of circumstances. When faced with adversity, choose love as your guiding light, responding with compassion, empathy, and understanding, and watch as love transmutes fear into light and healing.

My daily thoughts....

Honor your journey; it has shaped your wisdom.

Your journey through life is a tapestry of experiences, lessons, and growth, each contributing to the wisdom and insight that resides within you. Honor your journey, embracing both the triumphs and tribulations, and recognize that every step has shaped you into the wise and resilient soul that you are today.

My daily thoughts....

Use stepping stones to overcome Challenges

Challenges are not roadblocks but opportunities for growth and evolution, paving the way for your success and empowerment. Shift your perspective, viewing challenges as stepping stones on your path to greatness, and approach them with courage, determination, and resilience, knowing that each obstacle conquered brings you closer to your goals.

My daily thoughts....

Trust in the unfolding of your destiny.

Your life is a masterpiece in the making, guided by the unseen hand of destiny and the wisdom of the universe. Trust in the divine orchestration of your journey, surrendering to the flow of life, and have faith that everything is unfolding exactly as it should, leading you toward the fulfillment of your highest potential and purpose.

My daily thoughts....

*Let go of attachments to outcomes;
trust the process.*

Attachment to specific outcomes breeds anxiety and discontent, clouding your ability to trust in the natural flow of life. Release the grip of attachment, surrendering to the inherent wisdom of the universe, and trust in the unfolding of the divine plan, knowing that everything happens in divine timing and for your highest good.

My daily thoughts....

Embrace the ebb and flow of life's energy.

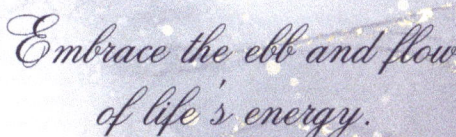

Life is a dance of ebb and flow, a rhythmic interplay of expansion and contraction, light and shadow, joy and sorrow. Embrace the inherent duality of existence, surrendering to the natural cycles of life's energy, and find peace in the knowledge that every peak and valley serves a purpose in your soul's evolution and growth.

My daily thoughts....

Practice mindfulness;
it brings clarity.

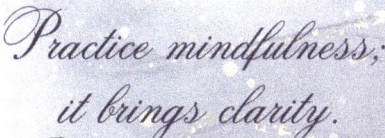

Mindfulness is the art of presence, a sacred practice of cultivating awareness and clarity in the present moment. When you practice mindfulness, you quiet the chatter of the mind, anchor yourself in the here and now, and attune to the beauty and richness of life unfolding around you with heightened clarity, focus, and presence.

My daily thoughts....

Celebrate your accomplishments, big and small.

Every achievement, no matter how big or small, is a cause for celebration and acknowledgment of your growth and progress. Take time to honor your accomplishments, basking in the glow of your successes, and affirming your ability to manifest your desires and intentions with dedication, perseverance, and hard work.

My daily thoughts....

Release the need for validation from others.

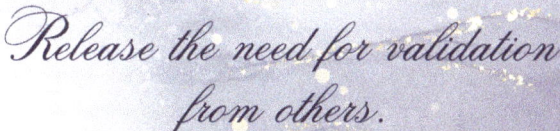

Your worth and value are intrinsic qualities that emanate from within, independent of external validation or approval. Release the need for validation from others, affirming your self-worth, and acknowledging your inherent value as a unique and precious expression of the divine.

My daily thoughts....

*Welcome vulnerability;
it nurtures connections.*

Vulnerability is not a weakness but a courageous act of authenticity, opening the door to deep connection, intimacy, and understanding in relationships. Embrace vulnerability, allowing yourself to be seen and heard in your truth, and cultivate connections based on honesty, empathy, and genuine human connection.

My daily thoughts....

Trust in the power of your dreams.

Your dreams are the whispers of your soul, guiding you toward your highest potential and deepest desires. Trust in the power of your dreams, believing in their validity and significance, and take inspired action to bring them to fruition, knowing that the universe conspires to support you in manifesting your heart's desires.

My daily thoughts....

Practice gratitude; it opens the door to abundance.

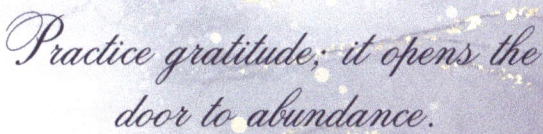

Gratitude is the key that unlocks the door to abundance, inviting blessings and opportunities into your life. When you cultivate a grateful heart, you shift your focus from scarcity to abundance, attracting more of what you appreciate and cherish.

My daily thoughts....

Embrace the cycles of life; they bring growth.

Life is a series of cycles, each offering opportunities for growth, transformation, and renewal. When you embrace the natural rhythms of life, you align with the flow of the universe, trusting that every phase serves a purpose in your evolution and journey toward wholeness.

My daily thoughts....

*Believe in your abilities
you are capable.*

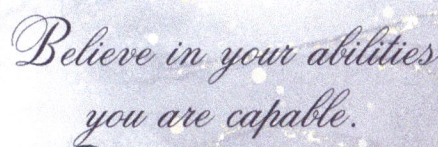

You possess within you a reservoir of untapped potential and limitless possibilities. Believe in your abilities, trust in your innate talents and strengths, and know that you are capable of achieving anything you set your mind to with determination, perseverance, and self-belief.

My daily thoughts....

Let go of the past the present is your power.

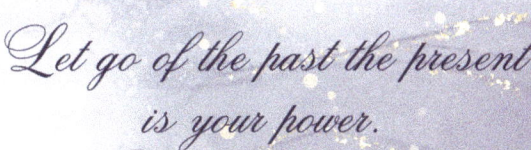

The past is a chapter that has ended, and the future is yet to be written. Release the grip of the past, freeing yourself from regrets and resentments, and embrace the power of the present moment. It is here, in the now, that you have the ability to create and shape your reality.

My daily thoughts....

Appreciate the journey, not just the destination.

Life is a journey, not a destination, and every experience along the way holds value and meaning. Take time to appreciate the beauty of the journey, celebrating each moment, lesson, and encounter as an essential part of your growth and evolution as a soul.

My daily thoughts....

Radiate love; it elevates the collective consciousness.

Love is the most potent force in the universe, transcending barriers and uniting all beings in a harmonious tapestry of interconnectedness. When you radiate love from the depths of your being, you contribute to the elevation of the collective consciousness, spreading light and healing to the world.

My daily thoughts....

Trust your inner guidance;
it knows the way.

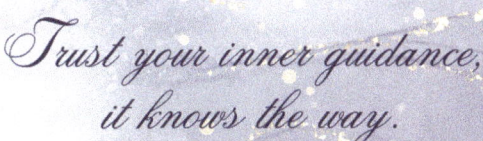

Within the depths of your soul lies a guiding light, a compass that points you toward your true north. Trust in the wisdom of your inner guidance, listening to the whispers of your intuition, and know that it will always lead you on the path of alignment, purpose, and fulfillment.

My daily thoughts....

Embrace the unknown; it holds infinite possibilities.

The unknown is not something to be feared but embraced, for it holds within it endless possibilities and potentialities waiting to be discovered. Step boldly into the unknown, surrendering to the flow of life, and allow yourself to be guided by the magic of serendipity and synchronicity.

My daily thoughts....

*Cultivate a grateful heart;
it attracts blessings.*

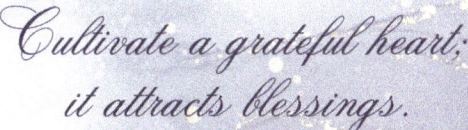

Gratitude is a magnet that draws blessings into your life, amplifying the abundance and joy that surrounds you. Cultivate a grateful heart, acknowledging the blessings, both big and small, that grace your journey each day, and watch as the universe responds with even more to be thankful for.

My daily thoughts....

Release the need for approval; validate yourself.

Your worth and value are not dependent on the approval or validation of others but stem from the inherent truth of your being. Release the need for external validation, embracing your uniqueness, and acknowledging your worthiness to live authentically and unapologetically as yourself.

My daily thoughts....

Surrender to divine timing; it's always perfect.

The universe operates in perfect synchronicity, orchestrating the unfolding of events in divine timing. Surrender to the flow of life, trusting that everything is happening exactly as it should, and have faith that the timing of your manifestations and desires is always impeccable.

My daily thoughts....

*Express your creativity freely;
it's your unique gift.*

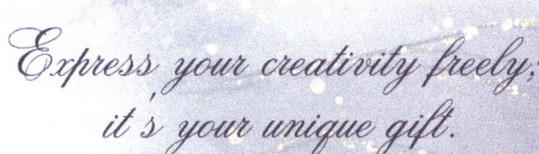

Creativity is the language of the soul, a divine expression of your unique essence and innermost desires. Allow your creativity to flow freely and uninhibitedly, trusting in the magic of your imagination, and honoring the creative impulses that arise within you as sacred gifts to be shared with the world.

My daily thoughts....

Trust in your resilience; you can overcome challenges.

Life is full of challenges and obstacles, but within you lies a wellspring of resilience and strength to overcome them all. Trust in your ability to rise above adversity, drawing upon the depths of your inner fortitude and courage to navigate life's trials with grace and resilience.

My daily thoughts....

Choose love as your guiding force

Let love be your compass in life, guiding your thoughts, words, and actions. Choose love in every moment, allowing it to lead you toward greater compassion, understanding, and connection with yourself and others. By choosing love as your guiding force, you align yourself with the highest vibration of the universe and open yourself up to infinite blessings and possibilities.

My daily thoughts....

Release self-limiting beliefs

Let go of beliefs that no longer serve you and instead embrace a mindset of unlimited potential and possibility. Release self-limiting beliefs about yourself, your abilities, and your worthiness, and trust in your inherent power to create the life you desire.

My daily thoughts....

Trust that you are where you need to be

Trust that everything is unfolding exactly as it should and that you are exactly where you need to be in this moment. Trust in the divine timing of your life's journey and have faith that the universe has a plan for you, even if it may not always be clear in the present moment.

My daily thoughts....

Express gratitude for both blessings and challenges

Cultivate a practice of gratitude by acknowledging and appreciating the blessings, both big and small, that grace your life each day. In addition to expressing gratitude for the positive aspects of your life, also express gratitude for the challenges and obstacles you encounter, recognizing that they too offer valuable opportunities for growth and transformation.

My daily thoughts....

See setbacks as setups for comebacks

View setbacks not as failures, but as opportunities for growth and resilience. Recognize that setbacks are often the catalysts for even greater comebacks, and that each setback you encounter is ultimately leading you closer to success and fulfillment.

My daily thoughts....

Cultivate a spirit of generosity

Cultivate a spirit of generosity by giving freely of your time, energy, and resources to those in need. Recognize that the more you give, the more you receive, and that acts of kindness and generosity have the power to create a ripple effect of positivity and abundance in the world around you.

My daily thoughts....

Find beauty in every moment

Train your mind to see the beauty that surrounds you in every moment, from the simplest of pleasures to the grandest of miracles. By finding beauty in the ordinary moments of life, you cultivate a sense of wonder and appreciation that enriches your experience and deepens your connection with the world around you.

My daily thoughts....

Surrender to the divine flow of life

Release the need to control every aspect of your life and instead surrender to the natural flow and rhythm of the universe. Trust that everything is unfolding exactly as it should and that the universe has a plan for you, even if it may not always align with your own expectations or desires. Surrendering to the divine flow of life allows you to experience greater peace, joy, and fulfillment in every moment.

My daily thoughts....

Embrace the power of positive affirmations

Harness the transformative power of positive affirmations to reprogram your subconscious mind and manifest your deepest desires. By affirming positive statements about yourself and your life, you align yourself with the energy of abundance and success, paving the way for greater happiness, prosperity, and fulfillment.

My daily thoughts....

Trust in the process of divine healing

Trust in the innate healing power of the universe to restore balance and harmony to your mind, body, and spirit. Whether you are facing physical, emotional, or spiritual challenges, trust that the universe has a plan for your healing and that everything is unfolding exactly as it should. Surrender to the process of divine healing and allow yourself to be guided toward greater health, wholeness, and well-being.

My daily thoughts....

Practice forgiveness

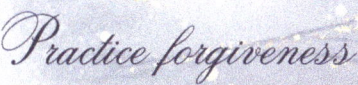

Release yourself from the burden of resentment and anger by practicing forgiveness toward yourself and others. Recognize that holding onto grudges only serves to weigh you down and prevent you from experiencing true freedom and peace of mind. By practicing forgiveness, you release the chains of the past and open yourself up to a future filled with love, compassion, and possibility.

My daily thoughts....

Connect with your inner strength

Draw upon the infinite well of strength and resilience that resides within you to overcome life's challenges and adversities. Trust in your inner strength to carry you through difficult times and empower you to rise above any obstacle that stands in your way. By connecting with your inner strength, you tap into a source of power that knows no bounds and allows you to navigate life's journey with courage, grace, and resilience.

My daily thoughts....

Release the need for external validation

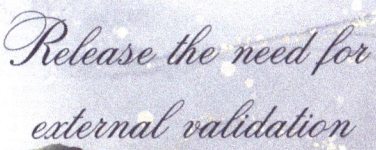

Free yourself from the need to seek validation or approval from others and instead validate yourself from within. Recognize that your worthiness and value are inherent simply because you exist, and that you do not need external validation to validate your worth. By releasing the need for external validation, you reclaim your power and affirm your own inherent worth and value.

My daily thoughts....

Trust that you are a co-creator of your reality

Recognize that you have the power to shape your reality through your thoughts, beliefs, and actions. Trust in your ability to manifest your desires and create the life you envision, knowing that you are a co-creator of your own destiny. By trusting in your creative power, you align yourself with the infinite potential of the universe and open yourself up to a life filled with abundance, joy, and fulfillment.

My daily thoughts....

Embrace uncertainty

Embrace the unknown with courage and curiosity, recognizing that uncertainty is a natural part of life's journey. Trust in the wisdom of the universe to guide you through uncertain times and know that every step you take, even in the face of uncertainty, is leading you closer to your highest good and greatest potential. By embracing uncertainty, you open yourself up to new opportunities, growth, and transformation.

My daily thoughts....

Cultivate a heart full of compassion

Cultivate a heart full of compassion for yourself and others, recognizing that compassion is the key to healing and transformation. Practice kindness, empathy, and understanding in all your interactions, knowing that even the smallest acts of compassion have the power to create profound shifts in the world around you. By cultivating a heart full of compassion, you align yourself with the highest vibration of love and create a ripple effect of healing and transformation wherever you go.

My daily thoughts....

Take inspired action toward your dreams

Take bold and decisive action toward your dreams and aspirations, knowing that action is the catalyst for change and transformation. Trust in your ability to turn your dreams into reality and take inspired action every day, no matter how small, toward making your dreams come true. By taking inspired action, you align yourself with the energy of manifestation and pave the way for the realization of your deepest desires and highest potential.

My daily thoughts....

Be kind to yourself on the journey

Treat yourself with the same kindness, compassion, and understanding that you would offer to a dear friend. Be gentle with yourself on the journey of life, knowing that you are doing the best you can with the knowledge and resources you have. By being kind to yourself, you create a nurturing and supportive inner environment that fosters growth, healing, and self-love.

My daily thoughts....

Radiate love

Let love be your guiding light and the driving force behind all your thoughts, words, and actions. Radiate love from the depths of your being, knowing that love has the power to heal, transform, and uplift both yourself and the world around you. By radiating love, you align yourself with the highest vibration of the universe and become a beacon of light and love for all who cross your path.

My daily thoughts....

Embrace the journey with an open heart

Approach life's journey with an open heart and an open mind, embracing each experience as an opportunity for growth, learning, and transformation. Trust in the wisdom of the universe to guide you along your path and know that every twist and turn in the road is leading you closer to your highest good and greatest fulfillment. By embracing the journey with an open heart, you open yourself up to endless possibilities and invite miracles to unfold in your life.

My daily thoughts....

Trust in the divine orchestration of your life

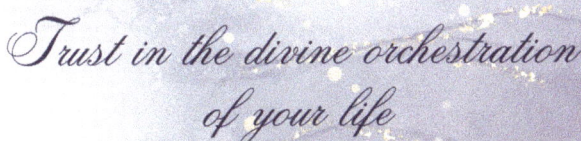

Have faith in the divine orchestration of your life and trust that everything is happening exactly as it should. Know that the universe has a plan for you and that everything you experience, both the highs and the lows, is leading you toward your highest good and greatest potential. By trusting in the divine orchestration of your life, you surrender to the flow of the universe and open yourself up to infinite blessings and possibilities.

My daily thoughts....

Know that you are loved beyond measure

Remember that you are unconditionally loved by the universe, Source, or whatever higher power you believe in, beyond measure or comprehension. Allow this deep knowing to fill you with a sense of peace, comfort, and security, knowing that you are always supported and held in the loving embrace of the universe. By knowing that you are loved beyond measure, you can move through life with confidence, grace, and gratitude, knowing that you are never alone and that you are always surrounded by love.

My daily thoughts....

Embrace change

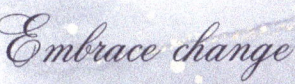

Embrace change; it leads to growth. Change is the essence of life, offering opportunities for personal evolution and expansion. Embracing change allows you to break free from stagnation, adapt to new circumstances, and discover hidden potentials within yourself. It opens doors to new experiences and perspectives, fostering resilience and a deeper understanding of life's mysteries.

My daily thoughts....

Seek balance

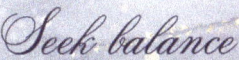

Seek balance in all aspects of life. Balance fosters harmony, ensuring that no area dominates while others languish, leading to a more fulfilled existence. By balancing your commitments, emotions, and energy, you create a stable foundation for personal growth and well-being. It allows you to navigate life's challenges with grace and equanimity, fostering inner peace and alignment with your true self.

My daily thoughts....

Trust your intuition

Trust your intuition; it's a powerful guide. Your intuition is a beacon of wisdom, offering insights beyond logical reasoning, guiding you along your path with clarity and purpose. It serves as a compass, directing you towards opportunities, decisions, and actions aligned with your highest good. Trusting your intuition enables you to navigate life's complexities with confidence, knowing that you are always guided by your inner knowing and divine guidance.

My daily thoughts....

Let go of fear

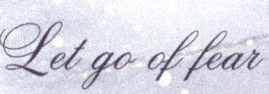

Let go of fear: it limits your potential. Fear constrains, inhibiting growth and preventing you from reaching your true capabilities. Release fear's grip and embrace boundless possibilities. When you release fear, you free yourself to step into your power, take risks, and pursue your dreams with courage and determination. By letting go of fear, you unlock doors to transformation and personal empowerment, allowing your true potential to shine brightly.

My daily thoughts....

Love unconditionally

Love unconditionally; it heals all wounds. Unconditional love is transformative, offering solace, healing, and renewal to even the deepest wounds of the heart and soul. It transcends judgment and expectation, embracing all beings with compassion, acceptance, and kindness. When you love unconditionally, you create a ripple effect of healing and harmony, nurturing connections and fostering a sense of unity and belonging in the world.

My daily thoughts....

Take a leap of faith

Take a leap of faith; miracles happen. Faith is the catalyst for miracles, propelling you beyond the confines of doubt and into the realm of endless possibilities where miracles manifest. When you take a leap of faith, you surrender to the unknown, trusting that the universe has a plan for you. It requires courage and trust in the unseen, but it opens doors to miracles, blessings, and divine interventions that exceed your wildest expectations.

My daily thoughts....

Find joy in the present moment

Find joy in the present moment. The present is where life unfolds, and within its embrace lies an abundance of joy waiting to be discovered, savored, and cherished. When you cultivate mindfulness and presence, you awaken to the beauty and magic of each moment, finding joy in simple pleasures and everyday miracles. By living in the present moment, you release worries about the past and future, allowing happiness and contentment to blossom within your heart.

My daily thoughts....

Patience is a virtue

Patience is a virtue; everything unfolds in divine timing. Trust in the rhythm of the universe, knowing that all things come to fruition at the perfect moment, according to the divine orchestration of time. Practice patience as you journey through life, surrendering to the natural flow of events and embracing the inherent wisdom of divine timing. In patience, you find peace, resilience, and a deeper understanding of the cyclical nature of existence.

My daily thoughts....

Listen to your inner wisdom

Listen to your inner wisdom; it knows the way. Within you resides a reservoir of wisdom, a guiding light that illuminates your path with clarity and purpose. Trust in its guidance, for it knows the way forward. Your inner wisdom speaks through subtle whispers, intuitive nudges, and gut feelings, offering insights that transcend logic and reason. When you listen to your inner wisdom, you align with your higher self and the divine intelligence of the universe, finding direction and clarity amidst life's uncertainties.

My daily thoughts....

Practice gratitude daily

Practice gratitude daily; it attracts abundance. Gratitude is a magnet for abundance, drawing forth blessings and enriching your life with joy, contentment, and a deeper appreciation for the beauty that surrounds you. When you cultivate a grateful heart, you shift your focus from scarcity to abundance, opening yourself up to receive the gifts of the universe. By practicing gratitude daily, you invite miracles and blessings into your life, creating a positive ripple effect that touches every aspect of your existence.

My daily thoughts....

Release what no longer serves

Release what no longer serves your highest good. Letting go of what weighs you down frees you to soar to new heights, unencumbered by the chains of the past and empowered to embrace the boundless possibilities of the present. When you release what no longer serves you, you create space for growth, transformation, and renewal. It requires courage and self-awareness, but the rewards are immense, leading to greater freedom, joy, and alignment with your authentic self.

My daily thoughts....

Forgiveness sets you free

Forgiveness sets you free; heal with love. Forgiveness is a transformative act of love, liberating you from the burdens of resentment and pain, and opening the door to profound healing, peace, and reconciliation. When you forgive yourself and others, you release the past and step into the present moment with an open heart and renewed sense of purpose. It is a gift you give yourself, allowing you to reclaim your power and embrace the fullness of life with grace and compassion.

My daily thoughts....

Your thoughts create your reality

Your thoughts create your reality; choose wisely. Your thoughts shape the world around you, manifesting your desires and sculpting your reality. Choose thoughts that align with your dreams and aspirations, for they have the power to create the life you envision. When you harness the power of positive thinking and visualization, you attract abundance, success, and happiness into your life, transforming your reality from within. Choose your thoughts with care, for they are the architects of your destiny.

My daily thoughts....

Connect with nature

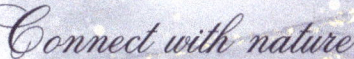

Connect with nature; it rejuvenates the soul. Nature is a source of profound healing and renewal, offering solace, inspiration, and a deep connection to the rhythms of life. When you immerse yourself in nature's beauty, you awaken your senses, quiet your mind, and rejuvenate your spirit. Whether it's a walk in the forest, a swim in the ocean, or simply basking in the sunlight, nature has the power to nourish your soul and restore balance to your being.

My daily thoughts....

Be kind to yourself

Be kind to yourself; you are deserving. Self-compassion is a cornerstone of emotional well-being, nurturing self-acceptance, resilience, and inner peace. When you treat yourself with kindness and understanding, you cultivate a nurturing inner environment that fosters growth, healing, and self-love. Remember to be gentle with yourself, especially in moments of struggle or self-doubt, for you are deserving of love, compassion, and forgiveness, just as much as anyone else.

My daily thoughts....

Trust the journey

Trust the journey, even in uncertainty. Life is an ever-unfolding journey, filled with twists, turns, and unexpected detours. Trust in the divine orchestration of your path, knowing that every experience, whether joyous or challenging, serves a greater purpose in your evolution. Embrace uncertainty as a catalyst for growth and transformation, surrendering to the flow of life with an open heart and unwavering trust in the unseen forces guiding your way.

My daily thoughts....

Open your heart to receive divine love

Open your heart to receive divine love. Love is the essence of the universe, flowing endlessly and abundantly to all who open themselves to its embrace. When you open your heart to receive divine love, you invite miracles, blessings, and synchronicities into your life, transforming your reality with its transformative power. Trust in the infinite capacity of your heart to give and receive love, knowing that it is the most potent force in the cosmos, capable of healing, uniting, and transcending all boundaries.

My daily thoughts....

Honor your emotions

Honor your emotions; they hold valuable lessons. Emotions are the language of the soul, offering insights into your inner world and guiding you along your path of self-discovery and growth. When you honor your emotions, you acknowledge their wisdom and allow them to flow freely, without judgment or resistance. Each emotion carries a valuable lesson and an opportunity for healing, leading you closer to wholeness, authenticity, and emotional well-being.

My daily thoughts....

Surrender control

Surrender control; let the universe guide you. Surrendering control is an act of trust and faith in the divine intelligence of the universe. When you release the need to control every aspect of your life, you create space for miracles to unfold, allowing the universe to work its magic in ways beyond your imagination. Surrendering control does not mean giving up or being passive; rather, it is about aligning with the natural flow of life and trusting in the inherent wisdom of the cosmos to lead you where you need to be.

My daily thoughts....

Embody compassion

Embody compassion; it transforms relationships. Compassion is the foundation of authentic connection and harmony in relationships, fostering empathy, understanding, and forgiveness. When you embody compassion, you see yourself and others with kindness and acceptance, creating a space for healing, growth, and mutual respect. It transcends judgment and ego, fostering deeper connections and a sense of unity with all beings. Embody compassion, and watch as your relationships flourish and thrive.

My daily thoughts....

Express your true self

Express your true self authentically. Authenticity is the key to living a fulfilling and meaningful life, aligning your actions with your values, passions, and inner truth. When you express your true self, you honor your uniqueness and gifts, inspiring others to do the same. It requires vulnerability and courage, but the rewards are immense, leading to deeper connections, self-acceptance, and a sense of purpose and fulfillment. Embrace your authenticity and shine your light brightly for the world to see.

My daily thoughts....

Find joy in simple pleasures; they are treasures.

Amidst the hustle and bustle of life, it's easy to overlook the simple pleasures that bring joy to our hearts. Take time to savor the beauty of life's small moments, finding delight in the everyday wonders that surround you, and treasure each moment as a precious gift to be cherished.

My daily thoughts....

*Connect with your inner child;
it brings joy.*

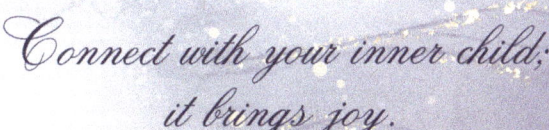

The inner child within you holds the key to boundless joy, creativity, and wonder. Reconnect with your inner child, embracing their playful spirit, curiosity, and imagination, and rediscover the joy and magic of life through the eyes of innocence and pure-heartedness.

My daily thoughts....

Honor your journey;
it has shaped your wisdom.

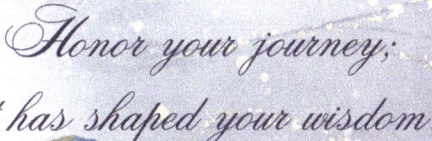

Your journey through life is a tapestry of experiences, lessons, and growth, each contributing to the wisdom and insight that resides within you. Honor your journey, embracing both the triumphs and tribulations, and recognize that every step has shaped you into the wise and resilient soul that you are today.

My daily thoughts....

Trust in the unfolding of your destiny.

Your life is a masterpiece in the making, guided by the unseen hand of destiny and the wisdom of the universe. Trust in the divine orchestration of your journey, surrendering to the flow of life, and have faith that everything is unfolding exactly as it should, leading you toward the fulfillment of your highest potential and purpose.

My daily thoughts....

*Let go of attachments to outcomes;
trust the process.*

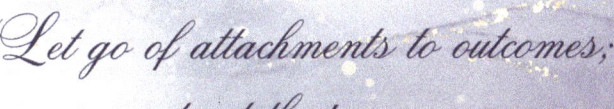

Attachment to specific outcomes breeds anxiety and discontent, clouding your ability to trust in the natural flow of life. Release the grip of attachment, surrendering to the inherent wisdom of the universe, and trust in the unfolding of the divine plan, knowing that everything happens in divine timing and for your highest good.

My daily thoughts....

*Embrace vulnerability;
it fosters connection.*

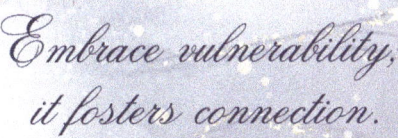

Vulnerability is not a weakness but a courageous act of authenticity, opening the door to deep connection, intimacy, and understanding in relationships. Embrace vulnerability, allowing yourself to be seen and heard in your truth, and cultivate connections based on honesty, empathy, and genuine human connection.

My daily thoughts....

Manifestation begins

Manifestation begins with a clear intention. Intention is the seed from which manifestation blooms, setting the course for your desires to manifest in the physical realm. When you set a clear and focused intention, you align your thoughts, emotions, and actions with your goals, creating a powerful energetic momentum that attracts your desires to you. Trust in the power of your intentions, and watch as the universe conspires to bring your dreams to fruition in miraculous ways.

My daily thoughts....

Let go of judgment

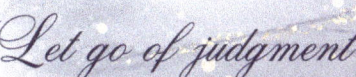

Let go of judgment; embrace acceptance. Judgment separates, creating barriers to understanding and connection, while acceptance fosters unity, compassion, and inner peace. When you release judgment, you embrace the diversity and complexity of life, opening yourself to a deeper sense of empathy, connection, and belonging. Let go of the need to label or categorize, and instead, embrace acceptance as the bridge that unites you with yourself and all beings in love and harmony.

My daily thoughts....

Your uniqueness is your strength

Your uniqueness is your strength; celebrate it. Your uniqueness is your greatest gift, offering a perspective and contribution to the world that no one else can replicate. When you celebrate your uniqueness, you honor your individuality and embrace the fullness of who you are. It empowers you to express yourself authentically, pursue your passions boldly, and make a meaningful impact in the world. Celebrate your uniqueness, and let it shine brightly as a beacon of inspiration and possibility for others.

My daily thoughts....

Nurture your body, mind, and spirit

Nurture your body, mind, and spirit. Your well-being encompasses more than just physical health; it extends to your mental, emotional, and spiritual vitality. When you nurture your body, mind, and spirit, you cultivate holistic wellness, balance, and vitality in every aspect of your life. Prioritize self-care, nourish your soul with positive experiences, and honor your body's needs with love and compassion. By nurturing yourself holistically, you create a foundation for a vibrant and fulfilling life.

My daily thoughts....

Seek the lessons in adversity

Seek the lessons in adversity; they lead to growth. Adversity is a teacher in disguise, offering valuable lessons, insights, and opportunities for personal growth and transformation. When you approach adversity with an open mind and a willingness to learn, you uncover hidden strengths, resilience, and wisdom within yourself. Embrace adversity as a catalyst for growth, knowing that every challenge you overcome brings you closer to your highest potential and greatest fulfillment.

My daily thoughts....

Cultivate a positive mindset

Cultivate a positive mindset; it attracts positivity. Your thoughts shape your reality, and a positive mindset cultivates an environment of optimism, hope, and abundance. When you focus on the good in life and maintain a positive outlook, you magnetize positivity, opportunities, and blessings into your life. Cultivate gratitude, optimism, and self-belief, and watch as your reality transforms into a vibrant tapestry of joy, success, and fulfillment.

My daily thoughts....

Be mindful of your words

Be mindful of your words: they shape your reality. Words carry immense power, shaping your thoughts, emotions, and experiences. When you speak with mindfulness and intention, you infuse your words with creative energy, manifesting your desires and shaping your reality. Choose words that uplift, inspire, and empower yourself and others, and witness the profound impact they have on your life and the world around you.

My daily thoughts....

Release self-doubt

Release self-doubt; you are capable and worthy. Self-doubt is a shadow that dims your light and undermines your confidence, but beneath its veil lies a wellspring of potential and worthiness. When you release self-doubt, you reclaim your power, recognizing your inherent value and capabilities. Trust in yourself, believe in your abilities, and embrace the truth that you are deserving of all the love, success, and abundance life has to offer.

My daily thoughts....

Connect with like-minded souls

Connect with like-minded souls: support each other. Connection is the essence of humanity, fostering understanding, empathy, and collaboration. When you connect with like-minded souls, you create a network of support, inspiration, and camaraderie that uplifts and empowers each member. Share your journey, exchange ideas, and celebrate each other's successes, knowing that together, you can achieve more and create a ripple effect of positive change in the world.

My daily thoughts....

Practice self-care

Practice self-care; it replenishes your energy. Self-care is a sacred act of nourishment and replenishment, honoring your body, mind, and spirit with love and attention. When you prioritize self-care, you restore balance, vitality, and resilience, ensuring that you show up as your best self in every aspect of your life. Make time for activities that nurture and energize you, and watch as your well-being flourishes, and your energy levels soar.

My daily thoughts....

Speak your truth with love and compassion

Speak your truth with love and compassion. Your voice is a powerful instrument of expression and transformation, capable of inspiring, healing, and uplifting those around you. When you speak your truth with love and compassion, you honor your authenticity and create space for open-hearted communication and understanding. Choose words that convey kindness, empathy, and respect, and let your truth reverberate with the healing power of love.

My daily thoughts....

See challenges as opportunities

See challenges as opportunities for transformation. Challenges are not obstacles; they are invitations to grow, evolve, and expand beyond your limitations. When you embrace challenges with an open mind and a courageous heart, you discover hidden strengths, insights, and possibilities within yourself. Reframe your perspective, see challenges as stepping stones on your journey, and seize the opportunity for growth and transformation that they offer.

My daily thoughts....

Your dreams are valid

Your dreams are valid; pursue them with passion. Your dreams are the whispers of your soul, calling you to express your fullest potential and live a life of purpose and fulfillment. When you honor your dreams and pursue them with passion and determination, you align with your soul's purpose and create a life that reflects your deepest desires and aspirations. Trust in the validity of your dreams, believe in yourself, and take inspired action to bring them to fruition.

My daily thoughts....

Share your light

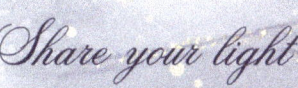

Share your light; it inspires others to shine. Your light is a beacon of hope, illuminating the path for others and igniting the flame of inspiration within their hearts. When you share your light with the world, you create a ripple effect of positivity, empowerment, and transformation, uplifting those around you and catalyzing change on a global scale. Shine brightly, share your gifts, and watch as your light inspires others to shine their brightest as well.

My daily thoughts....

Let go of attachments

Let go of attachments; true freedom lies within. Attachments are chains that bind you to the past, limiting your freedom and obstructing your path to growth and self-discovery. When you release attachments, you liberate yourself from the shackles of expectation and desire, finding freedom, peace, and fulfillment in the present moment. Let go of what no longer serves you, and embrace the boundless possibilities of a life lived with open hands and an open heart.

My daily thoughts....

Face fears

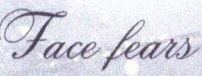

Face fears; they lose power in the light of courage. Fear is a shadow that looms large in the darkness, but when you face it with courage and conviction, it loses its power over you. When you confront your fears head-on, you reclaim your power and discover a reservoir of strength and resilience within yourself. Step boldly into the light of courage, and watch as your fears dissipate, leaving behind a trail of empowerment, growth, and transformation.

My daily thoughts....

Express gratitude

Express gratitude for both blessings and challenges. Gratitude is a practice that transcends circumstances, inviting you to find beauty and blessings in every moment, both joyful and challenging. When you express gratitude for your blessings, you amplify their abundance, and when you express gratitude for your challenges, you transform them into opportunities for growth and learning. Cultivate a grateful heart, and watch as your life becomes a radiant tapestry of joy and abundance.

My daily thoughts....

Surround yourself with positive energy

Surround yourself with positive energy. Energy is contagious, and the company you keep has a profound impact on your thoughts, emotions, and experiences. Surround yourself with people, environments, and activities that uplift and inspire you, nurturing a positive mindset and outlook on life. Choose positivity, cultivate optimism, and create a supportive and nurturing environment that empowers you to thrive and manifest your dreams with ease and grace.

My daily thoughts....

Align with your soul's purpose

Align with your soul's purpose; it brings fulfillment. Your soul's purpose is the guiding light that illuminates your path and infuses your life with meaning, passion, and fulfillment. When you align with your soul's purpose, you step into your power and live in harmony with the divine plan for your life. Trust in the wisdom of your soul, follow your heart's calling, and watch as your life unfolds with purpose, joy, and fulfillment beyond your wildest dreams.

My daily thoughts....

Be present in the moment

Be present in the moment: life unfolds now. The present moment is the gateway to peace, joy, and fulfillment, offering a sanctuary from the regrets of the past and anxieties of the future. When you cultivate mindfulness and presence, you awaken to the richness of life unfolding around you, savoring each moment with gratitude and wonder. Be here now, and let the magic of the present moment infuse your life with beauty, meaning, and boundless possibilities.

My daily thoughts.... 🪶

Connect with the divine through meditation

Meditation is a sacred practice that opens the doorway to the divine within, allowing you to commune with the infinite wisdom, love, and guidance of the universe. When you quiet your mind and open your heart in meditation, you enter into a state of deep connection and alignment with the divine, experiencing inner peace, clarity, and spiritual rejuvenation. Make meditation a daily ritual, and watch as your connection with the divine deepen.

My daily thoughts....

Release comparison

Release comparison; everyone's journey is unique. Comparison is the thief of joy, robbing you of the ability to appreciate and celebrate your own unique gifts and accomplishments. When you release comparison, you honor the beauty and authenticity of your own journey, embracing the uniqueness of who you are and the path you are meant to walk. Celebrate your individuality, and trust that your journey is unfolding exactly as it should, guided by the wisdom of your soul and the love of the universe.

My daily thoughts....

Find beauty in simplicity

Find beauty in simplicity; it brings inner peace. In a world filled with complexity and noise, simplicity offers a refuge for the soul, a sanctuary of peace, and tranquility. When you embrace simplicity, you let go of the unnecessary and focus on what truly matters, finding beauty in the ordinary and joy in the simple pleasures of life. Cultivate a life of simplicity, and watch as your heart expands with gratitude, contentment, and a deep sense of inner peace and fulfillment.

My daily thoughts....

Trust the process

Trust the process; the universe has a plan. Life is a journey of unfolding, guided by the unseen hand of the universe and the divine intelligence that orchestrates all things. When you trust the process, you surrender to the flow of life, knowing that everything is happening for your highest good, even if you cannot see it in the moment. Have faith in the divine timing of your life, trust in the wisdom of the universe, and watch as miracles unfold in perfect harmony with the grand design of existence.

My daily thoughts....

Take inspired action toward your goals

Take inspired action toward your goals. Action is the bridge between dreams and reality, transforming your aspirations into tangible results. When you take inspired action, you align your thoughts, emotions, and intentions with your goals, creating momentum and propelling yourself forward on the path to success. Trust in your abilities, follow your intuition, and take bold, decisive action toward your goals, knowing that each step you take brings you closer to your dreams.

My daily thoughts....

Cultivate a sense of wonder

Cultivate a sense of wonder; it fuels creativity. Wonder is the spark that ignites the fires of creativity, inspiring curiosity, exploration, and innovation. When you cultivate a sense of wonder, you see the world with fresh eyes, finding beauty and magic in the ordinary and extraordinary alike. Nurture your sense of wonder, and watch as it infuses your life with joy, inspiration, and limitless creative potential, opening doors to new possibilities and discoveries beyond imagination.

My daily thoughts....

Let go of perfectionism

Let go of perfectionism; embrace your imperfections. Perfectionism is a shadow that stifles creativity, undermines confidence, and robs you of the joy of self-expression. When you let go of perfectionism, you embrace the beauty of your imperfections, celebrating the uniqueness and authenticity of who you are. Embrace your flaws, make mistakes, and learn from them, for it is through imperfection that you find freedom, growth, and the courage to live life on your own terms.

My daily thoughts....

Choose love over fear in every decision

Choose love over fear in every decision. Love is the highest vibration in the universe, offering healing, transformation, and unity to all who embrace its power. When faced with choices, choose love over fear, knowing that it is the path to wholeness, connection, and divine alignment. Let love guide your thoughts, words, and actions, and watch as it transforms your life and the world around you with its boundless grace and compassion.

www.ingramcontent.com/pod-product-compliance
Lightning Source LLC
Chambersburg PA
CBHW062032290426
44109CB00026B/2602